JOSE ALTUVE

BASEBALL SUPERSTAR

BY BRIAN SANDALOW

Essential Library

An Imprint of Abdo Publishing
abdobooks.com

THIS BOOK CONTAINS
RECYCLED MATERIALS

Cover Photo: Leslie Plaza Johnson/Icon Sportswire/AP Images
Interior Photos: Keeton Gale/Shutterstock Images, 4, 74; Brett Coomer/Houston Chronicle/AP Images, 7; David J. Phillip/AP Images, 8, 11, 14, 90, 96–97; Eric Christian Smith/AP Images, 13, 47, 77, 86, 89; Mark J. Terrill/AP Images, 17; Ben Margot/AP Images, 18; Rob Tringali/MLB Photos/Major League Baseball/Getty Images, 21; Larry Goren/Four Seam Images/AP Images, 22; Shutterstock Images, 24–25; Matt York/AP Images, 28; Bill Mitchell/Four Seam Images/AP Images, 31; Pat Sullivan/AP Images, 32, 35, 44, 51; Dave Einsel/AP Images, 36; Erik Williams/Cal Sport Media/AP Images, 39; Charlie Riedel/AP Images, 42–43; Pat Sullivan/AP Images; Andy Clayton-King/AP Images, 48; Leslie Plaza Johnson/Icon Sportswire/AP Images, 54; Alex Brandon/AP Images, 57; Ann Heisenfelt/AP Images, 58; Rich Shultz/AP Images, 63; Juan DeLeon/Icon Sportswire/AP Images, 64, 69; Ben Margot/AP Images, 67; Tomasso DeRosa/AP Images, 71; Trask Smith/Cal Sport Media/AP Images, 72; AMF Photography/Shutterstock Images, 78–79; Michel Mond/Shutterstock Images, 80; Yi-Chin Lee/Houston Chronicle/AP Images, 83; Evan Agostini/Invision/AP Images, 84; Juan Carlos Hernandez/AP Images, 92; Prentice C. James/Cal Sport Media/Zuma Wire/AP Images, 95

Editor: Patrick Donnelly
Series Designer: Laura Graphenteen

LIBRARY OF CONGRESS CONTROL NUMBER: 2018967253

PUBLISHER'S CATALOGING-IN-PUBLICATION DATA

Names: Sandalow, Brian, author.
Title: Jose Altuve: baseball superstar / by Brian Sandalow
Other title: Baseball superstar
Description: Minneapolis, Minnesota: Abdo Publishing, 2020 | Series: Star athletes | Includes online resources and index.
Identifiers: ISBN 9781532119873 (lib. bdg.) | ISBN 9781532174704 (ebook) | ISBN 9781644940945 (pbk.)
Subjects: LCSH: Altuve, José, 1990---Juvenile literature. | Baseball players--United States--Biography--Juvenile literature. | Houston Astros (Baseball team)--Juvenile literature. | Sports--Biography--Juvenile literature.
Classification: DDC 796.35764092 [B]--dc23

CONTENTS

THE FALL CLASSIC

In October 2017, Jose Altuve and the Houston Astros faced the moment they had been waiting for. They had been the worst team in the league for three years running. Then, in 2015, an inexperienced Astros team made the playoffs but came up short. The team lost in the first round to the Kansas City Royals. This time, history was within reach.

A lot had changed over the years. The Astros went 51–111 in 2013, their third straight season with at least 100 losses. Two years later, Houston seemingly came out of nowhere to win 86 games and reach the American League (AL) playoffs as a wild card before running out of gas against Kansas City.

Along the way, Altuve went from being a curiosity to one of the best players in baseball. The Astros second baseman was the ultimate

Jose Altuve helped the Houston Astros make history in 2017.

underdog. Standing just five feet six inches (1.7 m), he was easy to overlook. But he quickly proved himself against the best in the game.

Altuve put together a season for the ages in 2017, hitting .346 with 24 home runs and topping 200 hits for the fourth straight year. He led baseball in Wins Above Replacement (WAR), a statistic that rates how valuable players are compared to their competition. He was the favorite for the AL Most Valuable Player (MVP) Award. Along with standout teammates George Springer, Carlos Correa, and Justin Verlander, he carried the high-flying Astros to the playoffs with 101 wins and an AL West Division title.

IN THE SPOTLIGHT

Altuve opened the playoffs in style. In Game 1 of Houston's series against the Boston Red Sox, he hit three home runs, becoming the tenth player to accomplish that feat in a postseason game. Two came against Boston ace Chris Sale, one of the toughest and most intimidating pitchers in the sport.

Altuve acknowledges the crowd after hitting his third home run of the day against the Red Sox.

"How good is Jose Altuve?" Astros manager A. J. Hinch said after the game. "It's incredible to watch him step up and be every bit the star that we needed today for sure. It's hard to describe in different ways."[1]

After watching Altuve's power display, teammate Springer said, "He makes sure he stays on top of his gym routine, whatever it is."[2]

The amazing performances continued for Altuve as the Astros moved closer and closer to the first championship in the team's 56-year history. Boston proved to be no match for Houston, with the Astros winning three of four games to breeze past the Red Sox. Altuve

HOUSTON'S PAINFUL 1980s

The Astros' 2017 playoff success was that much sweeter thanks to years of postseason frustration. Their first chance to reach the World Series came in 1980 when they won their first NL West title. That pitted them against the Philadelphia Phillies in a best-of-five series to reach the World Series. After splitting the first four games, the teams waged an epic battle in Game 5. Houston sent future Hall of Famer Nolan Ryan to the mound and led 5–2 after seven innings. But Philadelphia rallied to win the game.

Six years later, the Astros won the West again and needed to beat the New York Mets to win the NL pennant. With ace Mike Scott on the mound, Houston was nearly unbeatable and won the two games he started in the series. Trailing three games to two, the Astros believed if they won Game 6 of the series to force a decisive Game 7, Scott would pitch them to the World Series. Instead, they lost 7–6 in 16 innings and were eliminated one day before Scott's turn to pitch.

Astros manager A. J. Hinch, left, talks with Altuve before a game. Hinch rarely misses a chance to rave about Altuve's skills and commitment to the game.

played a key role in the victory, picking up eight hits in the series.

After defeating Boston, the Astros had to face the other big power from the AL East: the New York Yankees. New York entered the American League Championship Series (ALCS) with a powerful lineup. AL Rookie of the Year Aaron Judge slugged 52 home runs that year. Catcher Gary Sanchez added 33 more. But Altuve and the Astros were ready for the best-of-seven series. They won the first two games at home, both by a score of 2–1, with Altuve picking up five more hits. That left Houston just two wins shy of the pennant.

YANKEES FIGHT BACK

But momentum can shift at a moment's notice, and that's what happened in this series. Over the next three games in New York, the Yankees pounded Houston. They beat the Astros 8–1 in Game 3. Then the Yankees tied the series with a come-from-behind 6–4 win, scoring all six runs in their last two innings. Finally, New York's pitchers held Houston to just four hits in a 5–0 shutout in Game 5.

Altuve went 0-for-10 in the three losses. He wasn't the only player who struggled in New York. But he

The prospects of advancing to the World Series looked grim for Altuve, Carlos Correa, and the rest of the Astros when the Yankees won three straight in New York.

knew he had to step up if the Astros were going to save their season.

Back in their home ballpark, the Astros rallied. Verlander threw seven shutout innings in Game 6, and Altuve drove in two runs with a two-out single in the fifth inning. Houston led 3–1 entering the bottom of the eighth. Altuve stepped up to the plate to face New York's David Robertson leading off the inning.

Robertson was one of New York's toughest relief pitchers that year. He ran the count to two balls and two strikes. Then he threw a slider, a pitch that dives hard and away from a right-handed batter. But Altuve was ready for it. With a flick of his wrists he whipped his bat across the plate and hit the ball hard. It carried out to left field and over the fence for a home run. From there, Houston cruised to a 7–1 victory.

That set up Game 7, with the winner going to the World Series. And once again, Altuve played a key role. The Astros led 1–0 in the bottom of the fifth inning. Then with one swing of the bat, Altuve doubled their lead. He lashed a high fastball from New York's Tommy Kahnle on a line over the right field fence for his second home run in as many nights.

Houston scored twice more that inning and rolled to a 4–0 victory. When the last out of the game was made, Altuve said a silent prayer before celebrating with Correa, the team's shortstop. Altuve ended up jumping into the arms of the six-foot-four (1.9 m) Correa, who later explained the importance of the moment.

Altuve and Correa celebrate Altuve's big home run in Game 6 against the Yankees.

"It was very special. We're like brothers from another mother. We love each other so much, and we embrace each other and try to get better together," Correa said. "For us to accomplish something like this as teammates and double-play partners, it's extremely special."[3]

WORLD SERIES

For the second time in team history, the Astros were headed to the World Series. As the team prepared to face the National League (NL) champion Los Angeles Dodgers, the national media descended on Houston to learn more about this upstart team, and especially about its amazing second baseman.

"You run out of superlatives to say about him," former Astros star Craig Biggio told reporters. "It's really been fun to watch him evolve from when they signed him, and he kept fighting his way to get here. Then, all of a sudden, year in and year out, it's batting title after batting title and 200 hits after 200 hits and winning Gold Gloves and becoming the player that he is. Jose is a great player. He can do amazing things with a bat and a glove in his hand. But the thing I love the most

Altuve and his teammates celebrate their tense, seven-game victory over the Yankees in the ALCS.

about him is that he's so humble. He's an unbelievable player and a better person." [4]

It was no surprise that Biggio, a member of the Houston front office, held such beliefs about Altuve. But his opinion was shared by most people across baseball. Finally getting an extended chance to show off in October, Altuve was coming through as "MVP! MVP!" chants grew louder during his at bats in Houston's Minute Maid Park.

The chants didn't stop in the World Series. After the Dodgers took Game 1 in Los Angeles, Altuve and Correa homered back-to-back in the tenth inning of Game 2. The Dodgers came back to tie the score again, but Springer hit a two-run homer in the eleventh and Houston held on for a 7–6 win.

PIVOTAL MOMENT

The teams split the next two, and the Astros knew they needed to win Game 5. They didn't want to go back to Los Angeles trailing three games to two, leaving the Dodgers a win away from the title. But when Los Angeles took a 7–4 lead midway through Game 5, it looked like the Astros' championship hopes were in danger.

Altuve blasts a home run in the tenth inning of Game 2 of the World Series at Dodger Stadium.

But Altuve once again came to the rescue. With two runners on and two outs in the fifth inning, he hit a three-run homer that tied the score 7–7. He later drove in another run with a double, and Houston pulled out a wild 13–12 victory that put them within one win of a title.

"He's very, very underrated, believe it or not," Springer said of Altuve after the game. "But he's been clutch all year. He's been clutch his whole career. And I have the utmost confidence in him whenever he's up. He just kind

of does his job and goes home. But the guys in the clubhouse know who he is. The guys he plays against know who he is."[5]

Los Angeles won Game 6 at home 3–1, and the Astros once again found themselves playing a winner-take-all Game 7. And once again, the Astros came through, winning 5–1. The victory wrapped up their run from worst to first. It also completed Altuve's evolution from a good player known for his lack of height to one of the giants of the sport. During the 2017 playoffs, Altuve hit .310 with a .388 on-base percentage and seven home runs in 18 games. His 22 hits set a franchise playoff record. And he got to be forever part of World Series history by fielding the last out of Game 7.

GAME 5

No game symbolized the topsy-turvy 2017 World Series like Game 5. Played on October 29 in Houston, the Astros and Dodgers entered tied at two games each. The winner would have a 3–2 lead and need just a single game to win it all.

If only it were that simple. And Jose Altuve was in the middle of the action.

The game featured two of the sport's top left-handed pitchers, Houston's Dallas Keuchel and the Dodgers' Clayton Kershaw, and it was dominated by the hitters. In the fifth inning, the Astros trailed 7–4 but Altuve connected off reliever Kenta Maeda for a three-run game-tying homer.

Houston found itself behind again in the seventh inning, but Altuve's double in the seventh evened things up again. Finally, in the tenth, Houston won 13–12 on Alex Bregman's single. At five hours and 17 minutes, it was the second-longest game in Series history at the time.

Slugging outfielder George Springer, left, is one of Altuve's biggest fans.

Dodgers shortstop Corey Seager hit a ground ball to the right side of the Houston infield. Altuve, playing in short right field as part of a defensive shift, easily fielded the grounder in the grass, and his throw to first base beat Seager by several steps.

"The Houston Astros are world champions!" Fox Sports announcer Joe Buck proclaimed as the ball disappeared into first baseman Yuli Gurriel's glove.

Altuve and his teammates rushed the pitcher's mound to celebrate together. They had won the World Series, with Altuve's routine play wrapping up the historic moment.

By this point, it was clear that Altuve had cemented his place as one of baseball's best players. It wasn't a short journey to get there.

Altuve starts the celebration after throwing out Corey Seager for the final out of the 2017 World Series.

CLIMBING
THE LADDER

Jose Carlos Altuve was born May 6, 1990, in Maracay, Venezuela. As the story goes, Altuve's love of baseball came from his father, who enjoys sharing the story of the role baseball played in his son's birth.

On the day Jose was born, his father, Carlos, was watching a game at a stadium near the hospital where his mother, Lastenia, was preparing to give birth. When the time came for Jose to enter the world, his dad needed to be fetched from the ballpark.

"They ran from the hospital to the stadium to tell my dad, 'Hey, you have your kid already!'" Jose later recalled. "He said, 'OK, OK, let's go!' He was a big fan of baseball."[1]

In Maracay, that's not surprising. It's an area rich in talent that has produced numerous big league ballplayers. From a very young age, Jose aspired to

Jose Altuve was just 17 years old when he played his first season in the Houston Astros' minor league system.

The university baseball stadium in Venezuela's capital city, Caracas

be the next one. He could field, he could throw, he could run, and he could really, really hit.

There was just one problem: his height. Jose was about an inch shy of his current height when he began trying out for teams at age 16. He also didn't have a lot of weight on his frame. The Chicago Cubs, Los Angeles Angels, San Francisco Giants, New York Yankees, and others all were impressed by his skills. But in the end, they

couldn't picture Jose's body holding up to the demands of a 162-game season, so they all declined to sign him.

NOT GIVING UP

Determined, Jose kept trying out for teams and got a chance to impress the Astros at an event in Maracay. In front of Houston scouts, he was put through his paces. He ran a 60-yard dash, fielded, and hit, but he was sent home because he was too short.

A BASEBALL HOTBED

For a country with a population of roughly 31 million people, Venezuela has had an immense impact on the game of baseball. The country has produced nearly 400 major league players, the first coming in 1939 when Álex Carrasquel broke in as a pitcher for the Washington Senators.[3]

In 1956, the country's first Hall of Famer made his debut when Luis Aparicio appeared for the White Sox. Over the course of his 18-year career, Aparicio made 13 All-Star teams, won nine Gold Gloves, and won a World Series title as a member of the 1966 Baltimore Orioles.

And though Aparicio is currently the only Venezuelan in the Hall of Fame, that number will rise soon. Detroit Tigers slugger Miguel Cabrera, who in 2012 became the first player in 45 years to win the AL Triple Crown, is a shoo-in for the hall. Former Cleveland star Omar Vizquel, arguably the greatest fielding shortstop of all time, also has a strong case.

The Astros tryout continued the next day, and instead of staying home, Jose returned at the urging of his father, hoping the scouts would forget that he'd already been cut. He also hoped that Astros executive Al Pedrique, who was absent on the first day of the tryout, would be there and take the advice of scout Wally Ramos, who did believe in Jose.

Once again, Jose went through drills. He hit, fielded, and threw like a star. But this time, Pedrique was there. And with Ramos advocating for Jose, the Astros offered him the relatively small amount of $15,000 to sign.[2]

Quickly, Altuve showed Houston more than it thought it was getting. His first season in the Astros minor league system was 2007. He played with their Venezuelan Summer League team and hit .343. That was a good start, but it would be a different challenge once he began playing in the United States. In 2008, Altuve moved to Greeneville in the rookie-level Appalachian League. He batted .284 but struggled to hit for power. The next season, Altuve remained at Greeneville to start the season. But this time, he showed flashes of his potential, batting .324 with a .408 on-base percentage and 25 extra-base hits in just 45 games.

FAST RISE

From there, Altuve moved up the ladder quickly in the Astros' minor leagues. He finished 2009 with Tri-City in the short-season New York–Penn League. In 2010, he played his first full season in Class A, hitting .301 as a 20-year-old playing against considerably older competition.

The 2011 season saw more growth for Altuve. He began in high Class A with Lancaster, batting .408 in 52 games. Too good for that level, the Astros moved him to the Class Double-A Corpus Christi Hooks of the Texas League.

Just 21 and playing against some of the best prospects in

"I remember our first conversation. I asked him, 'Can you play?' He looked me in the eye and said, 'I'll show you.'"[4]
—Al Pedrique, Houston Astros special assistant who scouted Altuve

baseball, Altuve wasted little time showing he belonged. He batted .361 and was named to play on the World Team at the 2011 Futures Game, an exhibition played during the Major League Baseball (MLB) All-Star Week. It pits the best American prospects against those from around the globe.

"What he does on the field, it's just incredible," said Detroit Tigers third-base prospect Francisco Martinez, Altuve's teammate at the Futures Game. "The little man can hit. It's that simple. That little man can hit."[5]

But Altuve didn't want to be known solely as a little guy who could hit. He wanted to be a star big leaguer and a big part

OLD FRIENDS

They were born four days apart in a baseball-crazy country. It's only fitting that Jose Altuve and Royals catcher Salvador Perez would be friends.

Two of the best current players from Venezuela, Altuve and Perez were teammates in youth baseball, traveling to other countries to represent their home. They've also been American League teammates in the All-Star Game and instrumental pieces in their respective franchises' championship success.

"He always believed in himself, and I always knew he'd make it all the way to the majors," Perez said of Altuve. "He works hard, he plays hard."[6]

Altuve also had praise for Perez when the two were all-star teammates for the first time.

"I always knew he was gonna be here," Altuve said. "When he was 16, he already looked like a major leaguer. Actually, when he was 13 he already looked like a big leaguer. We had lots of fun together those days. We just worked hard and played hard and it was great. I love being here with him."[7]

Altuve represented the Astros on the World Team at the 2011 MLB All-Star Futures Game.

TWO SHORT SECOND BASEMEN

Altuve admired Boston Red Sox star Dustin Pedroia. Like Altuve, Pedroia is an undersized second baseman who overcame his stature to become one of the best in baseball. Both players are known for their aggressive hitting, hard-nosed defense, and fearless baserunning.

"He does everything the right way," Altuve said. "And he's been in the league longer than me—and when I was in the minor leagues he was one of my favorite players. He still is and he knows that."[9]

Pedroia is listed at 5-foot-9 (1.8 m) and has carved out an impressive career in baseball. He was the 2007 AL Rookie of the Year, won the 2008 AL MVP Award, and was a key figure in Boston's World Series titles in 2007 and 2013.

"To play the same position as Dustin Pedroia—former MVP, World Series, everything he has accomplished—I feel really proud to be like that in the same game and play against him," Altuve said.[10]

of the Astros' future, regardless of his stature.

"I know that everywhere that I go, people talk about [my size]," Altuve told reporters at the time. "But that's something that doesn't bother me a lot. It just pushes me to keep on playing. We have a lot of short guys in the big leagues, and I want to be one of them."[8]

At the end of the 2011 season, Altuve was named Houston's minor league player of the year and was the second baseman on Baseball America's minor league all-star team. However, he would not get a chance to repeat those honors the next season. He would be too busy playing at a higher level.

Altuve was a star at the plate and in the field for the Class-A Lancaster JetHawks in 2011.

EARLY BREAKTHROUGH

The 2011 Houston Astros were one of the worst baseball teams of all time. They went 56–106, becoming the first team in franchise history to lose more than 97 games in a season. But one positive of the season was the emergence of Jose Altuve.

Many players spend at least one year at the Triple-A level before they are called up to the major leagues. Altuve joined the Astros directly from Double-A on July 19, 2011. Houston had traded its starting second baseman, and the Astros needed somebody to play every day and develop for the future. That person was Altuve, who had clearly outgrown the minor leagues.

"The Astros are almost certainly rushing Altuve," a writer at NBCSports.com said. "He's just 21, and it's not at all likely that he's ready to hit for power in the majors. Still, he's the most intriguing

Jose Altuve grins during his major league debut on July 20, 2011.

position player they've developed since [former Astros outfielder] Hunter Pence, and given that the Astros are in need of a little excitement, it's not too surprising that they chose to give him a look."[1]

FIRST GAME, FIRST HIT

By this point, Altuve had established himself as a prospect, but whether he would become a standout major leaguer was still anyone's guess. Early on, he showed he might stick around for a while. In his July 20 debut, Altuve collected his first big league hit when he singled to right field off the Washington Nationals' Tyler Clippard.

That hit, while nothing spectacular, helped Altuve get off to a strong start. He opened his career with hits in seven straight games and homered for the first time on August 20.

Altuve connects for his first major league hit in the ninth inning of his Astros debut.

But there was nothing routine about his first home run. Facing the San Francisco Giants' Madison Bumgarner in the first inning at Minute Maid Park, Altuve hit a high fly ball to deep left-center field. Giants center fielder Cody Ross stopped short of the wall and let the ball bounce high off the warning track.

Altuve charged around the bases as the Giants outfielders tracked down the ball. Third base coach Dave Clark gave Altuve the sign to stop. But the rookie didn't break stride as he rounded third and headed for home. When San Francisco shortstop Mike Fontenot's throw home sailed wide, Altuve scored standing up for his

AN ALL-STAR FIRST

Altuve is one of the best hitters in baseball. That's not an opinion but a fact. He destroys bad pitching. He handles good pitching without a problem, too. Except for the All-Star Game. That hasn't been a place where Altuve succeeds.

Entering the 2018 MLB All-Star Game, Altuve had zero hits in eight at bats in the Midsummer Classic. Not very Altuve-like. And after striking out in his first at bat of the 2018 game, Altuve slumped to 0-for-9. Finally, in the fifth inning, he singled off the Philadelphia Phillies' Aaron Nola to end his All-Star drought. A player who had achieved everything else in baseball smiled from ear to ear after getting a hit in an exhibition. He asked for the ball as a keepsake, and his AL teammates cheered the moment.

"It felt weird," Altuve said. "It felt like I got my first big league hit or something like that—something I'd never done before, get a hit in an All-Star Game. But it feels good, and it was a good experience."[3]

With Astros fans cheering him on, Altuve crosses home plate after his first major league home run, an inside-the-park shot against the Giants.

CHECKING THE TRIPLE-A BOX

Altuve's resume isn't lacking much. He's a World Series champion, an AL MVP, a batting champion, and one of the best players in baseball. But before August 20, 2018, Altuve never had a hit at Triple A.

In 2011, Altuve was called to the Astros from Double A. He established himself as an everyday player in Houston so quickly that he never had to return to the minor leagues. In 2018, Altuve missed nearly a month with right knee soreness. When he was healthy enough to play again, he was sent to Triple-A Fresno for a short stint to sharpen his skills before returning to the Astros. He played only one game in Fresno, but Altuve took advantage of his chance to check another box. He singled during the game. And he kept that baseball, too.

"I got two 'first hits' this year—All-Star and Triple A," Altuve said. "I'm really proud."[4]

first big league home run. He earned a standing ovation from the crowd, who appreciated his hustle during a losing season.

The 2011 season ended on a down note for Altuve as he hit just .209 in September. However, his .276 average for the season was respectable, and he gave the Astros no reason to think they would need to look elsewhere for their second baseman of the future.

"When I came here last year in the beginning everything was good, but like half of the season they started throwing pitches that I didn't want and I kept swinging," Altuve said of his transition to the major leagues. "When I went back home, I started thinking about adjustments. [Opposing pitchers] made that

Before long, the sight of Altuve spraying hits to all fields became a regular occurrence at Astros games.

THE LONG AND SHORT OF IT

How much does a batter's height affect hitting ability? It depends on whom you ask. Professor Alan Nathan thinks the answer is: not much.

"You're trying to get the bat at the right place at the right time with as high a bat speed as possible," said Nathan, professor emeritus of physics at the University of Illinois. "Getting the high bat speed requires strength. Having a compact swing helps you do that. Having more weight also helps you do that, provided you know how to utilize that weight properly."[6]

Altuve's swing is indeed compact. His stroke is quick and direct to the ball with little wasted motion.

"He's got plenty of strength, and the thing that he does is he puts himself in good position to hit," former Astros hitting coach Mike Barnett said. "He's got a very good knack for being able to stay inside the baseball and use his hands."[7]

Yet, the question about whether all those assets can overcome size is still an open one. "This is a physical game, and you have to be able to hit the ball hard and drive the ball," said John Mallee, a former Astros hitting coach.[8]

adjustment and now it's time for me to do it."[5]

TAKING A STEP FORWARD

Altuve responded in 2012 by improving his batting average to .290. He also cut down on his tendency to swing at bad pitches, drawing 40 walks for a respectable .340 on-base percentage. With just seven home runs, he wasn't hitting for much power yet, but Altuve's speed and overall performance made him the highlight of an otherwise dreary season. He even made his first all-star appearance, going 0-for-1 during July's MLB All-Star Game at Kansas City's Kauffman Stadium.

"We've always felt he was mature beyond his years,"

Houston manager Brad Mills said. "But when you're in a situation where you're seeing him make adjustments from at-bat to at-bat, from pitcher to pitcher, that's been really impressive."[9]

Altuve also was part of one of the most curious moments in baseball history. On May 1, he batted against New York Mets pitcher Jon Rauch. An early-season matchup between a rising young hitter and a journeyman reliever wouldn't normally draw much attention. But this one stood out because Rauch is six feet 11 inches (2.1 m) tall. The height disparity between Rauch and Altuve is believed to be the biggest gap between a pitcher and batter in baseball history.

"I think most of the people like . . . Derek Jeter and Alex Rodriguez. They're pretty tall and they can do everything. But as a scout, you have to give credit to a little guy, too. See what they have. Who knows? See what they can bring to the table."[10]
—Jose Altuve on giving a chance to players who don't have the body of the ideal athlete

Rauch retired Altuve on a line out, but that was only a small part of the story. If anything, the moment turned a brighter spotlight on the Astros' budding star.

Altuve tries to turn a double play in the ninth inning of the 2012 All-Star Game in Kansas City.

"Why doubt this guy?" Mills said. "He's been able to do everything he has wanted to do in baseball, so who am I to doubt him? If I do that, he's going to go prove

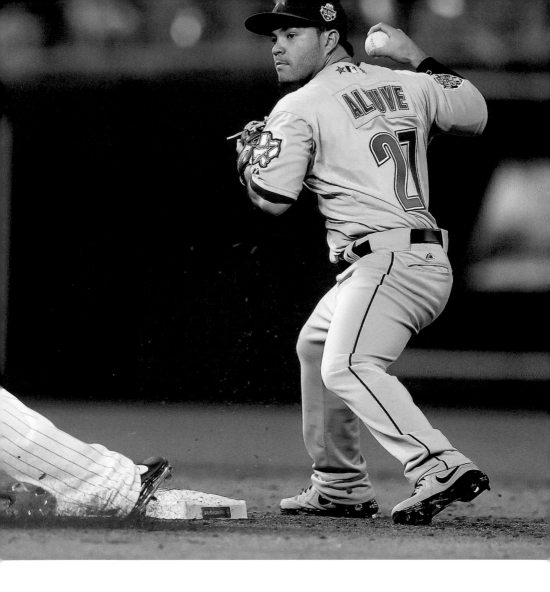

me wrong just like he's proven everybody else wrong his entire career. More power to him. God bless the guy. Let him just keep going."[11]

PERSONAL IMPROVEMENTS, **TEAM STRUGGLES**

When Jose Altuve signed with the Astros in 2007, the team was coming off the most successful period in its history. In the previous ten years, the Astros had made the playoffs six times. In 2004, they advanced to the NL Championship Series before losing to the Saint Louis Cardinals in seven games. And in 2005, Houston made it all the way to the World Series for the first time. The Chicago White Sox won the title in a four-game sweep, but it was still a banner year for the Astros.

But by 2013, Houston was in the middle of a complete franchise teardown. The 2011 Astros lost 106 games. The next year, they lost 107 games. And in 2013, after MLB moved them to the American League, the Astros lost 111 games. They

Jose Altuve makes a sliding play in 2013. He was a rising star even as the Astros were mired at the bottom of the standings.

had the worst record of any MLB team in each of those three seasons.

Yes, the Astros were bad. They were losing games at a historic rate and seemed to be years away from contention. However, positives could be found. One was Altuve, who was beginning to show the traits that would make him a star.

"Everything I do, I'm trying to do 100 percent, trying to do it pretending I'm playing," Altuve said, explaining how he prepares mentally for competition. "I don't overthink it. But you have to think, 'OK, they're doing this to you.' That's part of your plan. That's part of what you're going to take to home plate. You can't take too many things in your head, like, 'Oh no, he's going to throw a curveball or breaking ball.' I'm going up there ready to swing. I try to just simplify all the information I have, try to be aware of breaking balls, but try to keep [to] my plan."[1]

In 2013, Altuve's offensive numbers dipped a bit. He batted .283 with five home runs, with fewer doubles, triples, and walks than he had the year before. Yet his

Altuve lays down a bunt in a 2013 game against the Los Angeles Angels.

swing was showing signs of turning into something special.

"He has a quick, compact swing, and when he makes good contact the sound is not the deep *thunk* you hear when power hitters connect but a satisfying click," a *Sports Illustrated* writer noted.[2]

The Astros wanted to make sure they kept the owner of that swing in their organization. In July, they signed Altuve to a four-year extension worth $12.5 million.[3]

"Jose has quickly become the face of the franchise in less than two years, and we are excited to keep him here for many years to come," general manager Jeff Luhnow said at the time.[4]

BIG DREAMS

Jose Altuve's life story seemed like perfect fodder for an inspirational movie. In 2015, that came to be.

Commissioned by the Astros, *Big Dreams: The Jose Altuve Story* premiered in Houston in April 2015. The documentary, which also aired on MLB Network and local Houston TV stations, tells the story of Altuve's rise from Maracay to become one of the best hitters in baseball.

"It means a lot that the Astros are recognizing all the work I've done, and it means you're doing pretty good," Altuve said. "You want to keep doing that all your career."[5]

The film was made by MLB Productions director/producer Danny Field, who noted the role Jose's father played in Jose's childhood and how important it was to tell that part of the story.

"Jose hit it out of the park, but that is where the story crystallized for me—the pride [Carlos Altuve] has for his son and in the love that both his parents displayed," Field said. "Having a father express admiration for his son is rare, but it's perfect for their relationship."[6]

Altuve reacts to being called out on strikes in 2013.

LEARNING THE LANGUAGE

It would have been difficult for Altuve to become the face of the franchise if he hadn't been so eager to learn English. That desire dates back to his time in the minor leagues, when he always tried to make sure to have a US-born player as a roommate.

Altuve is clearly a gifted learner and has benefited from a dedicated program inside the Houston organization to teach English to players from other countries. He speaks his second language fluently and often gives compelling interviews on camera in English.

That attitude has rubbed off on teammate Alex Bregman, who took it upon himself to learn Spanish so he could communicate better with some of his teammates.

"We come from other countries without knowing English, and we come here and we have to learn the language," catcher Juan Centeno said. "I think [what Bregman is doing] is very important for the team's relationship, for communication on and off the field."[7]

After three straight seasons with at least 100 losses, even the optimistic Altuve had to wonder when it was going to turn around in Houston.

There was one downside for players learning English, however. They were able to understand all the heckles and insults opposing fans would yell at them.

"It was funny, because I would get upset," Astros minor league manager Rodney Linares said of the taunting. "[Altuve] would always be like, 'Don't worry about it—I've been called small all my life.'"[8]

COMING THROUGH FOR THE COMMUNITY

In addition to his role as one of the team's biggest stars, Altuve also quickly became an important part of the Houston community. In 2013, he earned his first nomination for the Roberto Clemente Man of the Year Award, a leaguewide honor that recognizes "current players who truly understand the value of helping others." Teaming with the Astros Foundation's Community Leaders program and the Astros Youth Academy, Altuve worked with area youth and encouraged them to stay on the right path in life.

"I don't think too much about mechanics. I just like to go up there and swing. It's more than my swing, though. It's my mindset. I always go to home plate with a plan." [9]

—Jose Altuve

Altuve took his charitable initiatives to another level in 2017 when he earned his second Clemente nomination and introduced the Jose Altuve Foundation. Over the years, Altuve has raised money to help children fighting cancer, donated gloves and other baseball equipment to young players in Venezuela, and supported efforts to rebuild Houston after Hurricane Harvey devastated the city in 2017.

"Jose Altuve exemplifies what we're looking for in our Astros players, both in the way he plays on the field, and the way he conducts himself off of the field," Astros general manager Luhnow said.[10]

BATTING
CHAMPION

By 2014, Jose Altuve stopped being a curiosity. His game was getting noticed, not his height. Altuve was blossoming into more than a good player on a bad team. He was being seen as a great player on a rising team. That season, he became the first player in baseball history to be named an all-star for the same team in different leagues. And the Astros improved their record to 70–92, still a long way from playoff contention, but 19 games better than the previous season.

His improvement began in the off-season when, on the heels of signing his big contract extension, he dedicated himself to improving his physical fitness. Instead of playing winter ball in Venezuela, he spent most of the off-season in Houston, where his workout regimen included both cardio and agility training and exercises such as running up steep hills to strengthen his legs.

Jose Altuve receives his 2014 AL Silver Slugger Award, given to the best hitter at each position, in April 2015.

SWITCHING LEAGUES

The Astros switched from the NL Central to the AL West in 2013 to balance the two leagues at 15 teams apiece. That allowed MLB to hold interleague games all season long, rather than limiting them to certain periods during the schedule. It also gave the Astros a true in-state rival in the Texas Rangers, who play their home games in a suburb of Dallas. Now, instead of facing each other in six interleague games per year, the rivals square off 18 times per season as divisional foes.

And he took nutrition more seriously as well.

"He understood he needed to be in better shape," Astros bull pen catcher and fellow Venezuelan Javier Bracamonte said. "It impressed me how much he changed in one year. And also he learned how to eat. In the minor leagues he was used to eating [fast food]; now he stays away from junk."[1]

The results showed on the field in 2014 as Altuve established himself as one of the top hitters in the game. His batting average topped .300 on May 16, and it stayed above .300 for the rest of the season. A month later, he got red-hot at the plate for two and a half weeks. Altuve entered play on June 15 batting .318. Then, over the next 16 games, he had 31 hits in 66 at bats, a .470 stretch that raised his overall average to a season-high .347.

Altuve takes part in fielding drills during spring training in 2014. He showed up to Astros camp in the best shape of his life that year.

By the All-Star break in mid-July, Altuve led the AL with 41 stolen bases and was third in the league in hitting at .335. The Astros' second baseman played in his second straight All-Star Game, where he drove in a run with a sacrifice fly. That plate appearance came against a familiar foe, Washington Nationals pitcher Tyler Clippard, who gave up Altuve's first career hit.

Altuve showed no signs of slowing down in the second half of the season. He ended up leading the major leagues with 56 stolen bases. He also was the first player since 1917 to steal at least two bases in four straight games. And he was even better at the plate. Altuve set the

HOW MANY ALTUVES?

An "Altuve" is not an official measurement. You can't find a ruler that's broken up into Altuves. But in 2012, Altuves were all the rage with fans who are always craving quirky new statistics. And combined with baseball's strength on Twitter, it was only a matter of time before the popularity of Altuves spread.

During a broadcast, Houston TV announcers Jim Deshaies and Bill Brown described an Altuve home run using the term "Altuves." It's a made-up unit of measurement that is 65 inches (165 cm) long to match the height of Altuve (who is rumored to actually be 5-foot-5 rather than his listed height of 5-foot-6).

That prompted an Astros fan to create a website and Twitter feed that measures various things in Altuves. According to the calculator at howmanyaltuves.com, the Empire State Building is 268.4 Altuves tall, the Golden Gate Bridge is 1,657.9 Altuves long, and the center field fence at Minute Maid Park is 75.5 Altuves from home plate.

Altuve steals one of his league-leading 56 bases against the Minnesota Twins in 2014.

Astros' single-season record with 225 hits, the most in the major leagues in 2014. And he was part of an exciting race for the AL batting title that came down to the last day of the season.

FINAL-DAY DRAMA

Entering play on the final day of the season, Altuve was hitting .340, three points ahead of Detroit's Victor Martinez. To protect Altuve's lead, the Houston coaching staff decided to hold the young star out of the lineup that day against the New York Mets. That would make it harder for Martinez to pass Altuve, whose average couldn't drop below .340 if he didn't play.

But that decision was controversial. Altuve wanted to play. And Astros fans registered their disapproval on social media. They wanted to see their favorite player earn the title with his bat instead of watching from the dugout.

"Strikes get called a little higher on his chest than they might on someone else's. But it almost doesn't matter because he's got such good bat-to-ball skills that as long as the ball is anywhere near the strike zone, he's going to be able to put it in play."[2]

—Astros general manager Jeff Luhnow

Altuve and the fans got their wish. About a half hour before the first pitch, the Astros announced on Twitter that they were making a lineup change. Altuve would be in the lineup after all, batting second in the order against New York's Bartolo Colon.

In the top of the first inning, Altuve grounded into a double play, but he doubled in the third inning and singled in the fifth. He finished the day with those two hits in four at bats, his sixty-ninth multihit game of the season, establishing a team record. His average climbed to .341. Meanwhile, Martinez went 0-for-3 and fell to .335. The batting title belonged to Altuve, the first player in Astros history to lead the league in hitting.

"That means a lot," Altuve said. "That's something I've been working for, and I'm trying to help my team every day. And to win a batting title and being the first one in franchise history is pretty exciting to me."[3]

His teammates and coaches toasted him with champagne after the game. And the bat he used in the final game was sent to the Baseball Hall of Fame in Cooperstown, New York.

The day capped a season in which Altuve did more than set records. He also achieved all three goals that he and Astros hitting coach John Mallee set for him back in spring training: make the All-Star team, lay off the bad pitches (he struck out a career-low 53 times), and win the batting title.

"That caps off [Altuve] as a person, the hard work he put in," Mallee said. "He went out and finished the job. He did it on the field."[4]

Altuve rests before the final game of the season against the Mets at Citi Field in New York. He got two hits that day to clinch his first batting title.

PLAYOFFS

Even while the Astros were losing games at a historic clip, they were remodeling themselves for a bright future. In 2014, *Sports Illustrated* published a cover story on the franchise's reliance on advanced statistics to build itself into a contender. The headline on the cover proclaimed it to be the 2017 World Series champion, as if the event had already taken place. Little did anyone know how prophetic that issue would become.

For most of baseball history, teams tried to avoid saying they were rebuilding. They wanted to stay somewhat competitive while also preparing for the future, partially to keep fans interested in going to the ballpark and watching games on television. Major League Baseball tried to help bad teams improve faster by giving them more high draft picks and allowing them to spend more money to sign prospects. Some teams took advantage of that system and became more willing to tear down their rosters with the idea

CHAPTER SIX

Jose Altuve and the Astros made a surprise run to the playoffs in 2015.

THE ARTICLE

Sports Illustrated is arguably the most prestigious sports publication in the United States. It's attracted many of the nation's best writers and photographers, and for a time it dictated the country's sports conversation.

That's part of what made the June 30, 2014, cover so remarkable.

With then rookie outfielder George Springer on the cover, the magazine called the Astros "Your 2017 World Series Champions." The accompanying article broke down the methods the Astros used to evaluate and draft players such as high school pitcher Brady Aiken, whom they took with the first overall pick in the 2014 draft.

But unlike many of the predictions in the article, Aiken didn't work out. He never signed with Houston and through 2018 had yet to play in the major leagues.

of bottoming out in order to eventually get better.

That's what Houston was doing. And by 2014, there were signs the strategy was working. Altuve was blossoming, along with a young core of players that included George Springer, Carlos Correa, and Marwin Gonzalez. And it was becoming apparent Houston's decision to rip up the team at the beginning of the decade was going to pay off.

After improving from 51 to 70 victories in 2014, the Astros made another huge leap in 2015. In late April the Astros started a 10-game winning streak that put them in first place in the AL West. They stayed in first for most of the first half of the season, only

Playing their hard-nosed brand of baseball, the Astros took a seven-game lead in the AL West by early May.

PLAYING FOR HIS COUNTRY

Altuve is a proud Venezuelan. He also wants to test himself against the best players in the world in any competition. That's why it wasn't surprising that he played for Team Venezuela in the 2017 World Baseball Classic, an international World Cup–style tournament held every four years in March.

"That is the only opportunity you have to represent your country with the jersey that has Venezuela on the chest," Altuve said. "I think you're representing the country by the way you play here and the way you act [in the big leagues], but this time you're going to have your flag on your chest. That's going to be very important."[1]

The tournament also gave Altuve a chance to team with Miguel Cabrera. The Detroit Tigers first baseman has staked a claim as one of the greatest hitters in baseball history. He's also one of the most important figures in Venezuelan sports.

Altuve and the Venezuelan team fell short of winning the tournament. He batted .259 with one RBI in seven games and even shifted to third base when needed.

slipping to second place on the day before the All-Star break.

Houston and the Texas Rangers waged a battle for first place down the stretch. The Astros led the division by 1.5 games when they visited Dallas for a four-game series starting on September 14. Then the Astros' youth came back to hurt them at the worst possible time. The Rangers, a veteran team with many players who had been through a pennant race before, won all four games and took control of the division.

However, the Astros didn't collapse. They ended up going 86–76—a 35-win improvement in just two seasons—and held off the Los Angeles Angels and the Minnesota Twins to capture the second AL Wild Card spot.

Altuve is tagged out at the plate by Texas Rangers catcher Robinson Chirinos. The Rangers eventually caught and passed the Astros to win the AL West in 2015.

"We didn't have the results a couple of years ago that we wanted, but we worked hard to be at this point. Now we are the team that everybody wants to be," said Altuve, whose profile increased even more in 2015.[2] Fans voted him into the All-Star Game as the AL's starting second baseman. He continued to set franchise records, reaching

800 career hits quicker than any player in team history. He also won his first Gold Glove, an award given to the best fielder at his position in each league.

The AL Wild Card Game was a win-or-go-home contest against the New York Yankees. Altuve drove in a run in the seventh inning as the Astros won 3–0 at Yankee Stadium. That allowed the Astros to move on to the AL Divisional Series, a best-of-five matchup against the Kansas City Royals.

"We're going to have to earn a lot more wins to get where we want to get, but this team is pretty special," Astros manager A. J. Hinch said. "Let's see what happens."[3]

The Astros won two of the first three games, leaving them one win away from advancing to the AL Championship Series. Then in Game 4 at Minute Maid Park, Houston took a 6–2 lead into the eighth inning. The upstart Astros were just six outs away from clinching the series in front of their raucous home fans.

But their normally reliable bull pen let them down. The Royals rallied for five runs to take the lead. They added two more in the ninth inning to win 9–6. Back in Kansas City for Game 5, the Astros took a 2–0 lead in the second

Correa gives Altuve a lift as they celebrate defeating the Yankees in the 2015 AL Wild Card Game.

Altuve clearly had become a fan favorite in Houston by 2016.

inning, but that's all they managed at the plate. Kansas City's pitchers held the Astros to just two hits in a 7–2 win, ending Houston's magical season.

Altuve was one of many Houston starters to have a rough series at the plate. He hit just .136—three hits in 22 at bats—in the five games. But the table was set for an exciting 2016, with the Astros expecting to take the next step forward.

Instead, Houston took a step back. The Astros won just 84 games and finished third in the AL West. They missed the playoffs by five games. However, Altuve won his second batting title with a .338 average, collected his one thousandth career hit, and finished third in the AL MVP voting. But what happened in 2016 would soon be forgotten, and for all the best reasons.

"I'm really proud of everything we did. I'm proud of their effort, I'm proud of their character, I'm proud how we handled adversity. Everything about this team, I'm proud of."[4]

—A. J. Hinch after the Astros were eliminated from the 2015 playoffs

MVP AND CIVIC HERO

Some athletes never have a moment of glory. For others, it's a brief and fleeting moment of greatness that's gone almost as quickly as it arrives. But for Jose Altuve, his moment of glory lasted the entire 2017 season.

The 2016 season was disappointing for the Astros even though Altuve did well. The next year, even more was expected of both the player and team. And both delivered.

Altuve hit a career-high .346 to win his third AL batting title. He slugged 24 home runs and drove in 81 runs and quickly emerged as a favorite to win the AL MVP Award. For the month of July, he hit an unheard-of .485 and at one point hit an even .500 between June 27 and July 27.

"He hit .500 for a whole month this year," Astros catcher Brian McCann said in disbelief.

CHAPTER SEVEN

Jose Altuve took his game to another level in 2017.

JOSE THE FATHER

On November 1, 2016, Jose Altuve became a father. His wife, Giannina—whom Jose knew growing up in Maracay—gave birth to a daughter, Melanie. Up to that point, most of Altuve's life had been focused on baseball. Having a daughter was not just going to add more love but perhaps a little balance.

"I think she's going to help me to become a better player," Altuve said. "Because you need some time off from baseball. Like when you have a bad game or you end up playing really good, you go home and you need to chill out. Like, 'OK I don't want to know anything about baseball until the next day.'"[3]

"He's playing a different game. I did that in high school."[1]

By now, little could surprise Altuve's teammates. Some, such as ace pitcher Dallas Keuchel, had gone with him through the Astros' farm system and saw him grow and blossom. But even Keuchel didn't know Altuve was capable of reaching such heights.

"I didn't know that he was going to actually be *this* good," Keuchel said during the 2017 season. "I thought he was going to be an All-Star, but to win the MVP, which he should—and honestly, he should have been in the race the last three or four years—and I couldn't be happier for the guy, because he is an all-American dude."[2]

The team around him also flourished. Infielders Alex Bregman and Carlos Correa and ace pitcher Justin Verlander—acquired in an August 31 trade with Detroit—formed the core of one of baseball's best teams. The frustration and disappointments from 2016 were fading

Infielders Alex Bregman, Altuve, and Carlos Correa made winning fun in Houston in 2017.

away for the young Astros. But the city of Houston was about to face an even bigger challenge.

In late August, Hurricane Harvey hit Houston with 50 inches (127 cm) of rain and dangerously high winds. Floods washed away homes and businesses, and the city was tested in a way it never had been before.

An aerial photo shows massive flooding in Houston in the wake of Hurricane Harvey in August 2017.

Altuve and the Astros responded. They staged an epic postseason run that gave the Houston fans a welcome distraction from their woes. But more importantly, they stuck around after the season to help the city rebuild and recover from the devastating effects of the hurricane. After the season, Altuve and other players volunteered

for Habitat for Humanity, building homes to help people affected by the storm.

Altuve's impact was also huge for the eventual World Series champions. And it wasn't just his performance on the field.

A relief worker checks supplies at a shelter in Houston. People from all walks of life came together to help the victims of Hurricane Harvey.

"The more you get to know him, the greater you think he is," Keuchel said. "Because it's not just about his MVP-type talent. He's a leader in the clubhouse. He's a guy who can make you laugh at any point in time. He loves music; he's always singing and dancing."[4]

Yet there's no denying his contributions on the field, especially in 2017. Name a baseball award that he was eligible for, and Altuve probably won it. He was *Baseball America*'s Major League Player of the Year. The *Sporting News* named him its Major League Player of the Year for the second straight year. He won the Babe Ruth Award, given to the best player in the playoffs, and the Hank Aaron Award, given to the AL's best hitter. And he was named the Associated Press's Male Athlete of the Year.

But two awards stood out above all the others. On November 16, Altuve was named the AL MVP, beating out New York Yankees rookie Aaron Judge with 27 of a possible 30 first-place votes. Jeff Bagwell, who won the Astros' first MVP award in 1994, had high praise for Altuve.

"I can't think of anything better to cap off the year for us," Bagwell said. "Jose, he's all that's good in baseball. A kid that gives everything he has, has fun doing it, a total team player that makes it fun to watch baseball. It's exciting. He's just special."[5]

And on December 5, Altuve earned another honor. He and football player J. J. Watt of the Houston Texans were named *Sports Illustrated*'s Co-Sportsperson of the Year in the wake of their hurricane recovery efforts. Watt was honored for raising $37 million for charitable

DAVID VS. GOLIATH

The 2017 AL MVP race was a study in physical contrasts. In one corner was Altuve, who had to overcome his lack of size to become an elite baseball player. Opposing him was Aaron Judge, the hulking New York Yankees outfielder. Judge stands 13 inches (33 cm) taller and outweighs Altuve by nearly 120 pounds (54 kg). Beyond the size comparisons, the two have very different games: Altuve is known for being an excellent contact hitter with emerging power. Judge, while striking out plenty, hits some of the longest home runs in baseball.

In the end, Altuve's .346 batting average and stellar defense won out over Judge's 52 home runs and .422 on-base percentage. After the announcement, Judge tweeted a photo of the two of them standing together on the field along with his congratulations: "M-V-P!!! Nobody more deserving than you!! Congrats on an unforgettable 2017!!"[8]

organizations, while Altuve was credited for lifting the spirit of a damaged city.[6]

"Altuve was the joyous catalyst for one of the most unlikely World Series runs in recent memory," the magazine's editors wrote in explaining their reasons for honoring Altuve. "Championships don't save communities, and we should be careful to assign too much weight to their powers of healing. But what other event can bring a million-plus people together and provide a platform, however ephemeral, to cast aside the differences that drive so many of us to sports in the first place?"[7]

Altuve and Aaron Judge share a laugh during a game in July 2017. Altuve edged the Yankees' rookie slugger for the AL MVP Award that season.

As for Altuve, helping the people who cheer for him was a no-brainer.

"The city of Houston has treated me really good," Altuve said. "I felt at that time that I owed them something. So when they were having a hard time, I wanted to give something back to them."[9]

"He's just a very different man. His antennae is so filled with correctness and honoring his teammates, handling the fans, handling the organization."[10]
—Sports agent Scott Boras

Altuve and football star J. J. Watt, right, of the Houston Texans were honored for their contributions to the hurricane relief efforts.

BEST IN
THE GAME

Jose Altuve has nothing left to prove. Any questions about his height have been answered for good. Worries about whether he'd have enough power to become an elite player have been silenced.

The only questions remaining concern his place among the greats of the sport. Will he reach the milestone of 3,000 hits? Is there a Hall of Fame plaque in his future?

"His bat-to-ball skills are unbelievable," teammate Alex Bregman said. "He makes hard contact. He's fast and uses his speed. He's a pure hitter. That's what he was born to do. There's no doubt in my mind he'll get to 3,000 [hits]. No doubt. Everybody knows he'll do it. He's well on his way."[1]

Jose Altuve has become one of the best players in baseball at any position.

It's nice to be as respected by one's peers as Altuve is. But there's nothing in his makeup that would allow him to be satisfied with his status.

"I'm coming off the best year of my career, a season when I won the MVP and we won the World Series, and maybe at one point I thought, 'Maybe now that I have some experience everything will be easier,'" Altuve said in 2018. "But I come in this year and it's the same. You're still going up against very talented pitchers. You might hit the ball well and the right fielder makes a great play on you, or the shortstop. What I mean by this is I don't much believe in projections, because baseball is so hard."[2]

Baseball might be hard, but Altuve has made it look easy. His 2018 season was down by Altuve's standards. He had knee problems that caused him to miss 25 games and led

CONTRACT EXTENSION

Jose Altuve and the Astros have bonded. Together, they've accomplished incredible things and owe much of their success to each other. In March 2018, the two sides decided to stay together long term.

Altuve signed a contract extension that's expected to keep him in Houston until he turns 34. The deal was worth a reported $151 million, making him one of the highest-paid players in baseball.[3] That's pretty good for a guy who originally signed for a scant $15,000.

"My family and I have made Houston our home," Altuve said when he signed the contract. "I have great teammates and coaches and we all have the same goal, we want to work hard and we want to win. Last year was really fun, but it's in the past. I'm excited about what the future holds and I'm excited to be with the Astros for years to come."[4]

Altuve credits his daughter, Melanie, and his wife, Giannina, with helping him keep baseball in perspective.

to off-season surgery, and he had to settle for 169 hits. But his star was still shining brightly. He also showed his toughness during the 2018 playoffs, collecting nine hits in eight games while playing on a knee that likely would have sidelined other players. The Astros, who won

a team-record 103 games and the AL West title, swept Cleveland before losing to the Boston Red Sox in five games in the ALCS. But Altuve was as good as any player on the field.

"You're going to have to drag him off the field, and I applaud him for that," Astros manager A. J. Hinch said.[5]

Then again, it's not surprising Altuve would have a generous helping of toughness. Any list of the best players in baseball mentions Altuve, and he's emerged as the best second baseman in the game because of his attitude and work ethic, both on and off the field.

"I think in this game you will get as far as the fans let you go. I owe them a lot."[7]

—Jose Altuve

"We saw at the academy how enthusiastic he was about playing the game, how he cheered his teammates on," said Al Pedrique, the man who signed Altuve in Venezuela. "I would often talk to the English teacher and Altuve was always among the top five. Same thing with the work in the gym."[6]

Altuve played through a knee injury as the Astros lost to the Boston Red Sox in the 2018 ALCS.

All of that work has paid off. And it's made Altuve one of baseball's most popular figures. He received 4,849,630 fan votes for the 2018 MLB All-Star Game, more than any other player in the league.[8]

Altuve views his success as a credit to everybody who helped him along the way. His parents instilled things in him that are still there and dictate who he is. His friends and teammates growing up in Venezuela competed with him and encouraged him to get the most out of his skill, ignoring questions about his size. Pedrique trusted what he saw and convinced the Astros to give Altuve a chance to prove that his height wouldn't hold

A HERO BACK HOME

Since 2010, Venezuela has suffered through a crisis. A failing economy has led to hunger, disease, and a skyrocketing crime rate, leaving the country's citizens desperate for positives. Jose Altuve has been a light in that darkness.

Proud of his Venezuelan roots, Altuve has never forgotten where he comes from. In turn, the people of Venezuela view him as one of their greatest exports and an example to follow.

Not only is Altuve an example for the youth of the country; he's something for everybody from Venezuela. They can cheer for him, and while they might not forget about their problems, they'll at least have a diversion for a few hours.

"He's a hero, an example for all of the kids in baseball schools across the city," Edilyng Rodríguez said after the Astros won the 2017 World Series.[9] Rodríguez lives in Maracay, where groups of fans gathered to watch Altuve—their *pequeño gigante*, or "little giant"—and fellow Venezuelan Marwin Gonzalez help carry the Astros to victory.

Altuve held a baseball clinic for young players in his native Venezuela in 2017.

him back. And once Altuve was in the Astros' system, the franchise developed him and honed his skills. They gave him an opportunity to jump into the big leagues a little early and took a risk on him.

But in the end, the reason Altuve has succeeded is himself. He has the work ethic and the natural ability to make everything work. In the process, he's become an inspirational figure to people who have been told, for one reason or another, that they don't have what it takes to achieve their goals.

> *"He surpassed all our expectations. More than his hitting and speed, what I most liked about him was his intelligence and heart, and his drive and absolute faith in himself."*[11]
>
> —*Al Pedrique*

"I never doubted myself because I already had too many other people doubting," Altuve said. "I wanted to prove those people wrong. And not because one day I could tell them they were wrong. I wanted to prove them wrong for the guys behind me who are short, too. Guys who are not really strong, not really tall, guys who are 14 to 16 right now who are very small and want to get an opportunity."[10]

Young fans look up to Altuve.

Keeping it fun is important to Altuve, who celebrates an Astros victory with teammates George Springer, Josh Reddick, Carlos Correa, and Jake Marisnick.

"I know maybe after that happened to me," he continued, "scouts now will think twice before telling someone, 'You're not going to make it.' They're going to think, 'This guy is the same size as Jose, and if Jose made it, maybe one of these guys can make it, too.'

"If I open at least one door, two doors, three doors for guys behind me, I'm going to feel like everything that I did, it was because of this, and that will feel good."[12]

TIMELINE

1990
Altuve is born in Venezuela on May 6.

2007
Altuve signs with the Houston Astros after getting rejected by multiple teams because of his height.

2011
The Astros promote Altuve to the major leagues on July 19, even though he had never played in Triple A; on August 20, Altuve hits his first home run, an inside-the-park homer against the San Francisco Giants.

2012
In what's believed to be the greatest discrepancy in height between a pitcher and batter, Altuve faces six-foot-11 New York Mets pitcher Jon Rauch on May 1; in July, he represents the Astros in the MLB All-Star Game.

2013
In July, Altuve signs the first big contract of his career, a four-year, $12.5 million deal.

2014
Altuve clinches his first batting title by getting two hits in the season finale.

2015

Altuve is voted the AL's starting second baseman at the All-Star Game; following a win over the Yankees in the wild card game, the Astros are eliminated by the Kansas City Royals.

2016

Altuve becomes a father on November 1 when his wife, Giannina, gives birth to a baby girl.

2017

Altuve wraps up his season with a career-high .346 average; Altuve and the Astros win the pennant with a 4–0 win over the Yankees in Game 7 of the ALCS; the Astros win the World Series for the first time by beating the Dodgers; Altuve wins numerous postseason accolades, including the AL MVP Award; on December 5, he and football player J. J. Watt are named *Sports Illustrated*'s Co-Sportsperson of the Year because of their efforts in helping Houston recover from Hurricane Harvey.

2018

The All-Star teams are announced and Altuve gets the most votes among all players.

ESSENTIAL FACTS

FULL NAME
Jose Carlos Altuve

DATE OF BIRTH
May 6, 1990

PLACE OF BIRTH
Maracay, Venezuela

PARENTS
Carlos Altuve and Lastenia Linares

SPOUSE
Giannina Altuve

CHILDREN
Melanie Altuve

CAREER HIGHLIGHTS

- Altuve played in the 2011 Futures Game, representing the World Team.

- Starting in 2014, he recorded at least 200 hits in four straight seasons.

- Altuve's 2017 season was one of the finest for any player in baseball. He won a batting title by hitting .346, was named American League (AL) MVP, and helped the Astros win their first World Series.

- Through 2018 Altuve had won multiple awards:

  - 2017 AL MVP

  - 2017 AL Hank Aaron Award

  - 2017 *Sports Illustrated* Co-Sportsperson of the Year

  - Six All-Star Game appearances

  - Three AL batting titles

  - Two-time Roberto Clemente Award nominee

  - 2015 AL Gold Glove

CONFLICTS

Altuve had to overcome perceptions about his height and whether he would be durable enough to withstand a full season of professional baseball. He was placed on the disabled list for the first time in his career on July 29, 2018, due to right knee pain.

QUOTE

"It's really been fun to watch [Altuve] evolve from when they signed him, and he kept fighting his way to get here. Then, all of a sudden, year in and year out, it's batting title after batting title and 200 hits after 200 hits and winning Gold Gloves and becoming the player that he is. Jose is a great player."

—*Former Astros star Craig Biggio*

GLOSSARY

batting average
A measure of a batter's performance obtained by dividing the number of base hits by the number of times at bat.

bull pen
The area on a baseball field where relief pitchers can warm up; can also refer to the group of relief pitchers as a whole.

clubhouse
A locker room used by an athletic team.

contract
A binding agreement between two sides for payment in exchange for services.

double
A hit that allows the batter to advance to second base.

double play
A play that results in two outs.

homer
To hit a home run.

minor leagues
A lower level of baseball where players work on improving their skills before they reach the major leagues.

on-base percentage

A measure of a player's ability to reach base via a hit, a walk, or being hit by a pitch.

pennant

An American League or National League championship.

postseason

The playoffs, including the wild card round, divisional playoffs, league championship series, and World Series.

rebuilding

Stocking a team with young players in hopes of future success.

single

A hit in which the batter reaches first base.

triple

A hit that allows the batter to advance to third base.

wild card

A team that makes the playoffs despite not winning its division.

ADDITIONAL RESOURCES

SELECTED BIBLIOGRAPHY

Crasnick, Jerry. "Led by Jose Altuve, Astros' Journey to World Series Shows the Heart of a Champion." *ESPN*. 22 Oct. 2017. Web. 16 Apr. 2019.

Miller, Scott. "Once Ignored by MLB, 5'6" Superstar Jose Altuve May Now Be Its MVP." *Bleacher Report*. Oct. 5, 2017. Web. 16 Apr. 2019.

FURTHER READINGS

Holley, Joe. *Hurricane Season: The Unforgettable Story of the 2017 Houston Astros and the Resilience of a City*. New York: Hachette, 2018.

McTaggart, Brian. *100 Things Astros Fans Should Know & Do before They Die*. Chicago: Triumph, 2016.

Reiter, Ben. *Astroball: The New Way to Win It All*. New York: Crown Archetype, 2018.

ONLINE RESOURCES

To learn more about Jose Altuve, please visit **abdobooklinks.com** or scan this QR code. These links are routinely monitored and updated to provide the most current information available.

MORE INFORMATION

For more information on this subject, contact or visit the following organizations:

FITTEAM BALLPARK OF THE PALM BEACHES
5444 Haverhill Rd.
West Palm Beach, FL 33407
fitteamballpark.com

The spring training ballpark of the Astros can seat 7,700 for games. Fans can also observe workouts at six practice fields on the 160-acre complex.

MINUTE MAID PARK
501 Crawford St.
Houston, TX 77002
astros.mlb.com

This stadium is the home of the Houston Astros. It was built in 2000 and has been the home of the Astros ever since.

NATIONAL BASEBALL HALL OF FAME
25 Main St.
Cooperstown, NY 13326
baseballhall.org

The Baseball Hall of Fame is the definitive museum for baseball. There are plaques honoring each of the inducted players and figures of the game, plus interactive exhibits about the sport's history.

SOURCE NOTES

CHAPTER 1. THE FALL CLASSIC

1. "Altuve Hits 3 Homers, Astros Beat Red Sox 8–2 in ALDS Opener." *USA Today*, 5 Oct. 2017, usatoday.com. Accessed 25 Mar. 2019.

2. "Altuve Hits 3 Homers, Astros Beat Red Sox 8–2 in ALDS Opener."

3. Jerry Crasnick. "Led by Jose Altuve, Astros' Journey to World Series Shows the Heart of a Champion." *ESPN*, 22 Oct. 2017, espn.com. Accessed 25 Mar. 2019.

4. "Led by Jose Altuve, Astros' Journey to World Series Shows the Heart of a Champion."

5. Anthony DiComo. "Altuve Recaptures Postseason Magic Just in Time." *MLB*, 31 Oct. 2017, mlb.com. Accessed 25 Mar. 2019.

6. Brian McTaggart and Ken Gurnick. "Houston Strongest! Astros Rule the World." *MLB*, 1 Nov. 2017, mlb.com. Accessed 25 Mar. 2019.

CHAPTER 2. CLIMBING THE LADDER

1. Brad Kyle. "The Improbable Journey: Jose Altuve from Venezuela Sandlot to World Champion." *Runner Sports*, n.d., therunnersports.com. Accessed 25 Mar. 2019.

2. Kyle, "The Improbable Journey."

3. "Alejandro Carrasquel: The Man Who Opened the Door to Venezuela." *La Vida Baseball*, July 2018, lavidabaseball.com. Accessed 25 Mar. 2019.

4. Richard Justice. "16-Year-Old Altuve to Scout: 'I Just Want a Chance.'" *MLB*, 29 Apr. 2018, mlb.com. Accessed 25 Mar. 2019.

5. Alden Gonzalez. "Astros Prospect Altuve Not Short on Talent." *MLB*, 10 July 2011, mlb.com. Accessed 25 Mar. 2019.

6. Matt Snyder. "From Childhood Friends to AL All-Stars: Salvador Perez, Jose Altuve." *CBS*, 14 July 2014, cbssports.com. Accessed 25 Mar. 2019.

7. Snyder, "From Childhood Friends to AL All-Stars."

8. Gonzalez, "Astros Prospect Altuve Not Short on Talent."

9. Christopher Smith. "Astros' Jose Altuve: Boston Red Sox's Dustin Pedroia 'Was One of My Favorite Players' When I Played in Minors & 'He Still Is.'" *Masslive*, 4 Oct. 2017, masslive.com. Accessed 25 Mar. 2019.

10. Smith, "Astros' Jose Altuve: Boston Red Sox's Dustin Pedroia 'Was One of My Favorite Players.'"

CHAPTER 3. EARLY BREAKTHROUGH

1. Matthew Pouliot. "Astros Call Up 5-Foot-7 Second Baseman Jose Altuve." *NBC*, 19 July 2011, nbcsports.com. Accessed 25 Mar. 2019.

2. Tyler Kepner. "Outsize Production." *New York Times*, 19 Aug. 2014, nytimes.com. Accessed 22 Mar. 2019.

3. Chandler Rome. "First All-Star Hit Finally Comes for Jose Altuve." *Houston Chronicle*, 18 July 2018, houstonchronicle.com. Accessed 26 Mar. 2019.

4. Chuck Schilken. "AL MVP Jose Altuve Cherishes Ball from First Triple-A Hit, Which Came Sunday During a Rehab Stint." *Los Angeles Times*, 21 Aug. 2018, latimes.com. Accessed 26 Mar. 2019.

5. Kristie Rieken. "Second Baseman Jose Altuve Leading Astros." *Lubbock Avalanche Journal*, 4 May 2012, lubbockonline.com. Accessed 26 Mar. 2019.

6. Zachary Levine. "Astros' Altuve Measuring Up as Big-Time Hitter." *Houston Chronicle*, 21 June 2012, houstonchronicle.com. Accessed 26 Mar. 2019.

7. Levine, "Astros' Altuve Measuring Up as Big-Time Hitter."

8. Kepner, "Outsize Production."

9. Rieken, "Second Baseman Jose Altuve Leading Astros."

10. Kepner, "Outsize Production."

11. Jerry Crasnick. "Jose Altuve Just Keeps Showing Up." *ESPN*, 16 May 2012, espn.com. Accessed 26 Mar. 2019.

CHAPTER 4. PERSONAL IMPROVEMENTS, TEAM STRUGGLES

1. "Hitters to Emulate: Jose Altuve." *ESPN*, 1 Apr. 2015, espn.com. Accessed 26 Mar. 2019.

2. Emma Span. "Little Slugger." *Sports Illustrated*, 8 Dec. 2014, si.com. Accessed 26 Mar. 2019.

3. Dan Gartland. "Report: Jose Altuve Nearing Five-Year, $150 Million Extension with Astros." *Sports Illustrated*, 16 Mar. 2018, si.com. Accessed 26 Mar. 2019.

4. "Houston Astros Sign Jose Altuve through 2017." *USA Today*, 13 July 2013, usatoday.com. Accessed 26 Mar. 2019.

5. David Barron. "Astros Report: Early Returns Are Positive for Harris." *Houston Chronicle*, 16 Apr. 2015, houstonchronicle.com. Accessed 26 Mar. 2019.

6. Barron, "Astros Report."

7. Marly Rivera. "For Alex Bregman, a New Way to Communicate." *ESPN*, 31 Oct. 2017, espn.com. Accessed 26 Mar. 2019.

8. Evan Drellich. "How Astros' 5–6 Altuve Rose to Height of His Profession." *Houston Chronicle*, 3 Aug. 2014, houstonchronicle.com. Accessed 26 Mar. 2019.

9. "Hitters to Emulate."

10. Brian McTaggart. "Giving Back to the Community Is Important to Altuve." *MLB*, 19 Sept. 2013, mlb.com. Accessed 26 Mar. 2019.

CHAPTER 5. BATTING CHAMPION

1. Emma Span. "Little Big League: How Jose Altuve Became an Unlikely Batting Champ." *Sports Illustrated*, 17 Dec. 2014, si.com. Accessed 26 Mar. 2019.

2. Emma Span. "Little Slugger." *Sports Illustrated*, 8 Dec. 2014, si.com. Accessed 26 Mar. 2019.

3. Brian McTaggart. "Altuve Claims First Batting Crown in Astros History." *MLB*, 27 Sept. 2014, mlb.com. Accessed 26 Mar. 2019.

4. McTaggart, "Altuve Claims First Batting Crown in Astros History."

CHAPTER 6. PLAYOFFS

1. Brian McTaggart. "Altuve Proud to Represent Venezuela in WBC '17." *MLB*, 21 Feb. 2017, mlb.com. Accessed 26 Mar. 2019.

2. "Diamondbacks End Season with 5–3 Win over Astros." *USA Today*, 4 Oct. 2015, usatoday.com. Accessed 26 Mar. 2019.

3. Bryan Hoch and Brian McTaggart. "Dallas, Houston KO Yankees." *MLB*, 6 Oct. 2015, mlb.com. Accessed 26 Mar. 2019.

4. Brian McTaggart. "Astro-Nomical Rise for Houston in 2015." *MLB*, 25 Dec. 2015, mlb.com. Accessed 26 Mar. 2019.

CHAPTER 7. MVP AND CIVIC HERO

1. Tyler Kepner. "To Measure Jose Altuve, Just Watch Him Soar." *New York Times*, 24 Oct. 2017, nytimes.com. Accessed 26 Mar. 2019.

2. Kepner, "To Measure Jose Altuve, Just Watch Him Soar."

3. Kristie Rieken. "Altuve's Addition Provides Much-Needed Balance." *AP News*, 25 Feb. 2017, apnews.com. Accessed 26 Mar. 2019.

4. Scott Miller. "Once Ignored by MLB, 5'6" Superstar Jose Altuve May Now Be Its MVP." *Bleacher Report*, 5 Oct. 2017, bleacherreport.com. Accessed 26 Mar. 2019.

5. Brian McTaggart. "November Reign: Altuve Wins AL MVP Award." *MLB*, 16 Nov. 2017, mlb.com. Accessed 26 Mar. 2019.

6. "From the Editors: Why J. J. Watt and Jose Altuve are SI's 2017 Sportsperson of the Year Honorees." *Sports Illustrated*, 5 Dec. 2017, si.com. Accessed 26 Mar. 2019.

7. "From the Editors."

8. @TheJudge44. "M-V-P!!! Nobody more deserving than you!! Congrats on an unforgettable 2017!! @JoseAltuve27." *Twitter*, 16 Nov. 2017, twitter.com. Accessed 26 Mar. 2019.

9. "From the Editors."

10. Chandler Rome. "Agent Scott Boras: Jose Altuve Is 'Hope Diamond of Baseball.'" *Houston Chronicle*, houstonchronicle.com. Accessed 26 Mar. 2019.

CHAPTER 8. BEST IN THE GAME

1. Jose L. Ortiz. "Jose Altuve Cruising toward 200 More Hits, But It's Not That Simple: 'Baseball Is So Hard.'" *USA Today*, 10 May 2018, usatoday.com. Accessed 26 Mar. 2019.

2. Ortiz, "Jose Altuve Cruising toward 200 More Hits."

3. Dayn Perry. "Astros and Jose Altuve Reportedly Agree to Five-Year, $151 Million Contract Extension." *CBS Sports*, 16 Mar. 2018, cbssports.com. Accessed 26 Mar. 2019.

4. Chandler Rome. "Jose Altuve Officially Signs Long-Term Contract Extension with Astros." *Houston Chronicle*, 19 Mar. 2018, houstonchronicle.com. Accessed 26 Mar. 2019.

5. "Hinch Says Altuve Would Be Out with Injury in Regular Season." *Yahoo*, 18 Oct. 2018, sports.yahoo.com. Accessed 26 Mar. 2019.

6. Ortiz, "Jose Altuve Cruising toward 200 More Hits."

7. Emma Span. "Little Slugger." *Sports Illustrated*, 8 Dec. 2014, si.com. Accessed 26 Mar. 2019.

8. Brian McTaggart. "Top Vote-Getter Altuve among 6 Astros All-Stars." *MLB*, 8 July 2018, mlb.com. Accessed 26 Mar. 2019.

9. Samantha Schmidt. "Jose Altuve's World Series Triumph Gives Shattered Venezuela Something to Celebrate." *Washington Post*, 2 Nov. 2017, washingtonpost.com. Accessed 26 Mar. 2019.

10. Scott Miller. "Once Ignored by MLB, 5'6" Superstar Jose Altuve May Now Be Its MVP." *Bleacher Report*, 5 Oct. 2017, bleacherreport.com. Accessed 26 Mar. 2019.

11. César Augusto Márquez. "Meet Al Pedrique, the Scout Who Lied about Jose Altuve's Height." *La Vida Baseball*, Apr. 2018, lavidabaseball.com. Accessed 26 Mar. 2019.

12. Miller, "Once Ignored by MLB, 5'6" Superstar Jose Altuve May Now Be Its MVP."

INDEX

ABOUT THE AUTHOR

Brian Sandalow has written for multiple major news organizations, including the *Chicago Sun-Times*, the *Sporting News* and the Associated Press. He is the author of *Chicago: America's Best Sports Town*. In 2006, he appeared on *Stump the Schwab*, an ESPN sports trivia game show. He lives in Chicago with his wife.